China AI

How China will dominate AI and blockchain technologies

Chris Rynning

Research
Sindre Laksemo
Monica Liu

ISBN: 9781723862069

CONTENT

INTRODUCTION

This book is a short read providing you with a framework and reference on artificial intelligence (AI) and blockchain in China. It also touches on the most famous "applications" running on the blockchain "operating system," the bitcoin. Most importantly the book encourages you to learn what AI is and the impact its related technologies may have. You yourself will have to decide what to do about it.

The book is *not* contemplated to be the "definitive work" on Chinese AI, rather it summarize some of the current issues and conditions for AI in the "Middle Kingdom." I respectfully leave it to academia and nationwide experts to drill into details on technology, philosophy, statistics or regulations. Here you will find a snapshot on a topic that may carry you through a high level board meeting or set you up for an interesting dinner conversation.

In 2013, I published the book *"Little Streams, Big River"* on the Chinese economy with a deep dive into some of China's environmental challenges. The need for a "second edition" gnawed on me already the year after publishing, as China kept changing so much, so fast. An update was overdue almost from the moment it was published. This book may certainly not be more than a "yard stick" to see what was thought about Chinese AI late 2018, yet I hope the topic and questions asked will age well.

Let's first demystify what AI is.

AI is simply algorithms trying to predict outcome and learning from the same outcomes. Algorithms are step by step instructions or software codes that machines or humans can follow to preempt an action or react to an event. If you connect many algorithms together, then the result may be a product, a service or a task/decision made. Humans have always tried to predict outcomes, especially when calculating risk or making decisions. There has always been competition among tribes, nations or companies to make better decisions. AI can facilitate faster and better decisions.

Predicting outcome using models and computing power is also nothing new. In fact, we can trace the use of predictive, statistical models back for centuries. Thomas Bayes laid a foundation for today's AI in the 1750's with his theoretical, or maybe we can say "artificial," mathematical models. "Bayesian analysis" allowed for new information to be included in models, thereby updating our belief, also turning prior probabilities into so-called posterior probabilities.

Bayesian analysis now for example at the core of autonomous vehicles. Cars constantly receive data from sensors like cameras and lanes to update its location and status. The data collected from all the sensors are put into a Bayesian model. The software model then calculates fast and consistent actions. Sensor data will come from both internal factors, like the vehicles' own speed and external factors, like where are lanes or objects. The model then can rapidly forecast and change behavior for the next second in time, better than most humans.

Gathering data, predicting outcome and adjusting action using statistics and software coding, is artificial intelligence. Most students of statistics will have learned about Bayes. Indeed, in the 1990's I dragged myself with some difficulty through statistical and mathematical studies at the University of Chicago (Booth), not realizing the impact of what I was reading. AI demystified? Hopefully a little bit.

AI is everywhere *today*. AI suggests your Spotify playlist, recognize voice commands on your smart phone or predicts the risk and treatment of cancer. AI is only software codes after all. An unfortunate anchoring effect when thinking of AI is the threat of machines dedicated to eliminating human life on earth. The popular mind is anchored with blockbusters like Arnold Schwarzenegger's "Terminator" which leaves many thinking of AI as a destructive military force in the form of machines looking to extinguish the human race.

There is little evidence for this scenario, other than what is currently produced in Hollywood, including doomsday warnings from the likes of billionaire Elon Musk. I too certainly favor a cautious and regulated approach and development of AI, reducing the possibility of accidentally developing doomsday machines. So far, the benefits vastly seem to outweigh the current downsides, but more about that later.

China has fully embraced AI, from President Xi to its tech titans and its many citizens. A key argument in this book is that the Chinese people seem willing to arbitrate personal privacy for convenience. There will naturally be a debate whether this is by choice or no choice. My discussions with Chinese people indicate that it is not a contentious issue for most Chinese, and this author feels the same way. I do not much care that the government or tech companies know when my birthday is or what I bought online. I am willing to arbitrage this knowledge for the benefit of having suggestions made to me that I even did not know existed.

Imagine that you are feeling sad and gloomy. Even better: AI can detect a pattern that indicates you may *become* sad and gloomy. AI then sets off a range of measures to preempt your sadness. For depressed or suicidal people, such an AI effect could be lifesaving. Or imagine that you feel joyful and adventurous. AI may even be able to predict your imminent happiness, clear your calendar and recommend a range of activities that enhance your life.

An AI machine that you daily interact with is your mobile phone. Your little pocket mate may be your best friend or your worst enemy. Whatever you may think of that, it is most likely made in China and reshaping your life in fundamental ways. This author wants to focus on exploring, debating and developing AI that may benefit and prolong human life. From Spotify to autonomous cars, the author sees AI transforming everyday life the same way the industrial revolution changed the world in the 19th century, only this time originating in China.

And China versus the US? Eric Schmidt, former CEO of Google and executive chairman of its parent company, Alphabet, puts it like this: *"It's pretty simple. By 2020, China will have caught up. By 2025, China will be better than the US. By 2030, China will dominate the industries of AI."* Chances are he is right and that China got the future covered.

CHAPTER 1 – ARTIFICIAL INTELLIGENCE IN CHINA

In 2017, the local Beijing authorities could not understand why their public toilet paper spending was going through the roof in certain locations. Investigation led to the "discovery" of more or less organized groups raiding parks every morning for the daily new supplies of toilet paper. Immediate action was taken: Small rolls where replaced by industrial, larger rolls.

It turned out that the toilet paper thieves were doing even more rounds, pulling out large or small amounts of paper from the larger rolls, putting the paper in bags or inside their clothing. If anything, loss was either stable or went up. Personnel was dispatched to monitor and apprehend the "toilet paper gangsters" to little effect. The final answer was deploying AI with facial recognition and digitalizing the bathrooms to the amusement or irritation of the public.

To access public bathrooms, you now had to allow a facial picture of yourself. If you had within the nine previous minutes been to a bathroom in the vicinity, you would not be granted access again. The theft of toilet paper fell to near zero overnight. Lifting toilet paper is not a global problem, but no good for local public health or public service in general. Those who do not want the government to know they use Chinese public toilets, be forewarned. In fact, facial technology now is capable of following most people in urban centers near full time to provide full surveillance of your whereabouts.

Pervasive facial recognition solutions are possible in part because the cost of computing has come down dramatically, allowing for mass deployment of cameras, while processing capacity has increased exponentially. You most likely know Moore's law well. It stipulates doubling of computing power every 24 months. This exponential growth in computing power is why AI has become one of the hottest topics on the planet. Computer speed is now so fast that it is hard to compare with where we were, 15 years ago, not to say where we were in the 1970s. It is said that NASA landed on the moon with less computing power than that of a current pocket calculator. Another analogy is that if car's maximum speed would have improved at the same rate as computing power, then the fastest cars today would travel at *8 million times the speed of light*. That is pretty, pretty fast.

China aims at becoming the world's dominant player in artificial intelligence by 2030. This is government policy from Beijing. If you look at manufacturers of supercomputers in existence with high speed and their location, then China is well on its way. Chinese companies and China's government overtook the USA in 2017 as producer of supercomputers and has in 2018 decisively been pulling away. According to Forbes, in 2018 China has 206 of the top 500 supercomputer producers, while American corporations and the United States government designed and made only 124 of the supercomputers on the list. There are three Chinese companies on the top five list with "Lenovo" being number one, "Inspur" third and "Sugon" fifth. American companies "Hewlett-Packard" is second and "Cray" is fourth.

Protectionist matters and continuous trade conflicts with the USA will only spur Beijing on to become completely independent of the USA, also in supercomputing. This author's prediction is that the trade conflicts with the USA will hurt American companies disproportionately as they may not only be blocked from the Chinese market, but Chinese companies and governments will receive much more support, projects, and capital. This will have ring effects into other markets too, especially to South East Asia, Africa, and South America. Even

Europe may turn more towards China for supercomputing should trade conflicts persist.

In 2002, China had no supercomputer on the list. Today it is firmly in the lead. A sign of what impressive catch up China is able to make, and there is no evidence that China will stop its development here simply because it is now *leading* the list. Trade spats with the USA will in itself ensure that. It is not all bleak for the USA as they did reclaim the throne in 2018 for the fastest clocked supercomputer with "Summit," an IBM backed supercomputer at the US Department of Energy. Summit beat China's Sunway "TaihuLight," which had been ranked the world's fastest since it came into operation in 2016.

Doubt the intent, the plan and the ability for Beijing to execute on delivering long-term supercomputing infrastructure and AI? In the author's experience, don't. The financial capacity and political will to deliver in Beijing is unmatched by any other government. Russia may be too corrupt and too small with a GDP merely 10% of China. The Russian "bear" does not have the liquidity, nor critical mass and data. The US seems too polarized. With Washington DC in constant disarray, can republicans and democrats agree on anything anymore? Should NASA put all its eggs in Musk's basket? I doubt it.

China, for better and worse, is used to launch and administer mega projects, where public and private sectors cooperate. Projects such as the "High Speed Rail," "Three Gorges," "One Belt, One Road" and the remarkable building of "Shenzhen City" from a few hundred thousand people to a 20 million plus urban metropolis all show that China have track record and financial capacity to deliver on mega projects. There are uphill battles for China, do not get me wrong. China may be behind the USA on software development but catching up there too. On hardware,

China is starting to get a pretty decent domestic manufacturing base. Combining it all is complicated, but certainly not impossible.

Beijing is focused on developing AI and robotics, with a whole range of financial and academic support programs to follow up. As much as Beijing's focus and financing is instrumental, it is available Chinese data and the consumers' willingness to let companies and the government use that same data to make predictions and decisions, which is the "killer argument" in China's favor.

Chinese AI engines may simply become faster in making better and more efficient decisions, because of data advantages. While western politicians debate and consider data privacy, Chinese tech companies plough away with both regulative and capital support from all layers of the government. Combining a favorable regulatory landscape with mass scale, in combination with huge amounts of engineering students and a self-thought talent pool that no country can match. There is an exponential amount of data available in China, either from the use of WeChat or from chips/sensors in billions of "internet of things" markers. This data amount and liberal user access is key for China's privileged AI position.

Chinese tech companies Baidu and Alibaba also have generous and competitive cloud computing services available to its clients at low costs. This democratization of computing and storage power in China is another strong indicator of innovation enabling effects. Millions of users have been empowered and financed to use and store unusually large data amounts previously only controlled by governments and some large tech companies.

Alibaba, JD.com and Chinese e-commerce companies control nearly 42% of *global* e-commerce. Would it not be fair to expect these tech superstars to be leading innovators in payment, health, and entertainment? In fact, they already are. In urban China, shopping experience is hyper modern with omnichannel stores, personalized shopping experience, robots, and digital payment.

Consumers in China have leapfrogged technology and expect robots and machines to increase efficiency. They demand automation; they do not fear it. They want to eliminate factory work or anything that is dull, dark and dangerous ("3D"). Unions in China are not, in the same way, lobbying the government to protect laborers from robots or autonomous operators, unlike in the USA and Europe. The mentality seems different here. China and Beijing do not dwell on the *"Great 1950's or 1960's,"* like populists in America. In fact, the consensus seems to be that the 1950's and 1960's can be improved upon. Improved a lot. China expects roll out of robots and AI to be fast, now and convenient. If it also means reallocation and pain in the labor force, then so be it. No pain, no gain and eventually "we will get it right" seems to be the overriding attitude. There is technological optimism, not surprising maybe in a society dominated and built by engineers.

The era of arbitrating cheap labor and export oriented polluting manufacturing for economic gain is nearly over for China. Now follows an intense period where China will arbitrate the regulatory landscape and personal data laws to allow labor to be replaced by machine efficiency.

China does not *want* to manufacture in China. China is tired of its air pollution, dead rivers, and poor global reputation. Being associated with air pollution is not what Beijing, nor the Chinese people want. In addition, an estimated one million people are dying from air pollution related causes annually. It is real for the Chinese, statistics for others. The Chinese don't want to work in factories. If Africa and Michigan would like to manufacture and "be great again" that is their choice. That era is over in now vastly tech-driven China. The "China Dream" is to replace labor with advanced and innovative technology. China has left this 19th-century economic model, racing towards a future where tech and AI are enablers for longer and better life.

The geopolitical impact is important as China is outsourcing manufacturing labor to South East Asia and Africa. China have spent the last ten to twenty years to build emerging market ports, roads, factories and renew local water supply. Yes, they have backlashed in some locations and territories, but China also seems to have learned how to be non-interfering and bolster a local middle class. There is no other country in the world that can both finance and build global infrastructure, while in the process also creating literally billions of new consumers. This outsourcing allows, no, ...demands... rapid efficiency and tech development at home, as China re-think its international goals.

Global emerging markets with their emerging consumers are *not* developed by German, American or Japanese companies. They are mainly dominated by Chinese businesses and the Chinese government. The new factories built in Vietnam, Myanmar, and Indonesia are *not* built by Germans. They are nearly all built by Chinese. So what does this mean? It means additional captive markets and more data for Chinese companies. Not French or Swedish companies. The incentive to share data and emerging markets for the Chinese? Nil. China has 1.4 billion people, but I estimate the Chinese *"sphere of influence"* is nearer to 3 billion, counting Africa, South East Asia and large parts of South America. The Chinese led growth and investment abroad, is poorly reflected in official GDP data. When a Chinese state-owned company closes a polluting factory in Hebei province but opens a new one in Myanmar with local Chinese financing, it is unclear how this value is accurately reflected in official Chinese GDP data. It is nevertheless Chinese "owned" growth. It provides Chinese influence and dominance with geopolitical implications.

On top of an increasing "international influence sphere," China is by far the largest home market for technology in the world. You name it: mobile phones, internet users, mobile payment, renewable technology. China is the biggest market for almost anything you can imagine. A large home market also can provide Chinese companies which success at home, instant scale and chance of profits and liquidity abroad. China is a near fully connected 1.4 billion consumer market with one culture, one language and a desire to work hard to succeed. It follows that it would be naïve to think that China is not set up as an epicenter of future tech development. In fact, the combination of access to large-scale market, talent pool and nearly unlimited capital nearly guarantee rapid tech development.

Not all projects or companies will succeed, and return on total capital invested may be low for many years and for many institutions. Low returns for some may not matter much in an environment where the winner takes it all, in particular since return on capital may not be related to market success or market share. You will see this in current macroeconomics in China today. For example, many analysts and commentators think that the debt bubble in China will cause China to collapse. It will likely not. China is unlikely to collapse because of debt, because nearly all Chinese debt is domestic or internal, from SEOs to local governments or Chinese households to Chinese banks or other Chinese entities.

Non-performing loans and bad projects/debt in China will be written off, with serious consequences to the investors that invested in the wrong projects. There is historic precedence for write offs in China, and there is no reason to believe it will change now. The write offs will be fatal for some entities, but for most merely uncomfortable. Why? Well, the asset side is rarely given the same focus as the liability side of the balance sheet in Chinese state owned enterprises and governments. Chinese savings, disposable income or non-public assets for governments, corporates, and households are sky high by most international standards. Chinese companies and governments, with some notable exceptions obviously, are all putting away and covering assets for a rainy day. Moreover, China has not started the "privatization" wave that western economies undertook from the 1970's, raising capital to refinance and build the country. China has a lot of assets on its balance sheet which is not properly priced or converted to cash. In my experience, Chinese corporates and households have put away unknown, but large reserves of liquidity for a rainy day.

Taking the European and US debt crises as an example, where the USA owe money to China, or Greece owe money to Germany, it is a different thing for a Chinese state entity to owe money to another state entity. It is like your one pocket owes money to your other pocket, not somebody else. This is a dramatically improved situation; would you not agree?

This *"right pocket owes left pocket"* situation, allow China to simply write off the debt from one pocket to another, or writing off non-performing assets, or printing more money with the main consequence that "return on investment" falls since exchange rates and interest rates are politically "fixed." Falling or negative return on capital is not "life-threatening" to anyone and may even be expected "when you are building a country" and don't want to depend on access to foreign capital or resources. Most analysts get this dynamic wrong. Hence, don't worry about an imminent hard landing because of debt in China, it will not happen the way Dr. Doom claims it will. That does not mean that China does not have rocks in the ocean. It has, but it is not debt. At the same time, AI may accelerate GDP growth, counterbalancing slower growth rates. Global consulting firm McKinsey predicts that automating workplaces with AI could add 0.8 to 1.4 percentage points to GDP growth annually, and that China will be in the lead to do so.

Hard work

There is a saying in China that *"if you want to get rich, you have to get up before the sun rises."* The saying reflects generations of incredibly hard working rice farmers in China, having had to get up early and go to bed late to ensure that there is the right amount of water flowing in the rice field, the right crop is growing and all more or less fully attended to by hands.

There is no room for laziness in the Chinese agrarian culture, where the vast amount of its people were employed as late as 30-40 years ago, with many still trying to get out. This is the current Chinese parent generation that has learned to work hard, and they may see the opportunity to get ahead, both on a local level and now increasingly on a global scale.

China is tired of being laughed at. They want a "come back," they want to think big, they will work harder than most and have access to capital. I cannot but conclude that China has the upper hand also on work ethics and risk taking. From "tiger moms" to "entrepreneurship dads" Chinese children may be spoiled, but most of them are also pushed, driven and encouraged to work hard, long and with the best.

China, the USA and the rest

AI in China is not left to the private sector to develop, or to local tech titans like Jack Ma, Pony Ma or Robin Li. As mentioned above, President Xi intends for Beijing to have a piece of the action both for economic and for geo-political reasons. AI has been on the mind of Zhongnanhai, China's "White House," for years. China's State Council announced China's "Next Generation Artificial Intelligence Development Plan" in 2017 with the goal of becoming the leading global AI innovation hub by 2030.

The audit and consulting firm PricewaterhouseCoopers published a report where they projected that AI deployment will add $15.7 trillion to the global GDP by 2030, with China accounting for about $7 trillion of that total, compared to only $3.7 trillion in gains in the US. Underlying this is that China in 2017 accounted for 48 percent of the world's total AI startup funding, compared to 38 percent in the US.

There is an unofficial race towards singularity between the west, the east and the rest. The race is hard to define, and the contenders are a bit unclear. Most experts seem to define the polar opposites here as US, China and the "rest" holding Europe, Japan, Korea, and Russia. In this mix are individuals, companies and maybe some paralegal organizations. Some of the individuals focused on AI are known, like the tech titans named above. Surely Alphabet, Facebook, Apple, Amazon, Tencent, Baidu, and Alibaba are all companies in the race. Among nation states, it is blurrier. Everybody in the west, especially western media and politicians, seems to regard the investment and development of artificial intelligence in China as the biggest contender. To others, it seems like an understatement.

Experts widely disagree with what it means for the human race to reach a form of "singularity," but the winner of such a race could reasonably expect to positively shift economic status and prosperity for its people or shareholders, at the disadvantage to other nations. Until the machines take over everything and kill us all? So, how advanced is China's AI research and commercial status? Our reading suggests that China has the most *valuable* AI companies in the world and that global experts mid-2018 believe that China is probably just a small, insignificant step behind the leading American companies in developing AI, if behind at all. Valuation of AI related companies as such is not an indication of development stage in a country widely criticized for its unreal valuations, but as a minimum seems to suggest what kind of capital or liquidity that could be available for Chinese companies in the AI sector. Experts whom we talked to seem to disagree on the data pointing to who is in the lead, the USA or China. The USA seems to have more companies, and more AI categorized talent and have historically been investing more in the sector. Others point to the fact that China don't categorize AI engineers the same way, indicating underreporting of talent in China and that historic investment numbers are obsolete. The argument is that China has caught up and passed the US. To us, it seems quite even in 2018, but with the future tilted towards China.

How we got here
AI developed as a phenomenon in science fiction and technology departments during the 1950's and 1960's mainly in the USA. Criticized at the time in the Soviet Union as a *"bourgeois reactionary pseudoscience,"* both China and the (then) Soviet Union had virtually no artificial intelligence research. Deterioration of relations between the Soviet Union and China through the 1960's set development in China further back and it was not until Deng Xiaoping implemented reform and opened up the country that we can see rapid technological progress in China.

President Xi's recent focus on technology development is having a new positive effect on the local Chinese technology and research community. While Xi has accelerated AI and tech innovation from 2017, our reading suggests that the first Chinese policy that mention of AI was in February 2006, when the Chinese State Council, *"China's cabinet,"* released a national *"Long-Term Plan for the Development of Science and Technology."* This was a plan where various government departments were asked to formulate policies to help establish a national innovation system centered on enterprises up to the year 2020.

Again, we noticed the Chinese willingness to think and plan for the longer term. This plan included tax incentives for innovative companies and a "soft introduction" of measures to protect intellectual property. These early steps *"made a bed"* for later AI planning, such as the release of the *"12th Five-Year Plan for Intelligent Smart Manufacturing"* in 2012. In this plan, we can start to see the different Chinese ministries' fingerprints for an AI plan, targeting smart industrial robots and Internet of Things ("IOT"). The plan talks of technologies that integrate a large amount of information from a specific field and uses that information to make better decisions than humans in specific situations to serve specific goals.

Global concerns on machines replacing labor are not equally mirrored in labor intensive China. New jobs in China are not created in agriculture, transportation or old manufacturing. New jobs are created in services like health, education and financial sectors with higher efficiencies, still with needs of human intelligence and creativity. Chinese academics openly debate the "accelerated law of returns" and whether it will usher in "singularity" much earlier than expected, eliminating human jobs or the human race, whichever is worse. The most optimistic Chinese academics hold like the well-known researchers Carl

Frey and Michael Osborne of Oxford University that every "revolution" destroyed some professions such as well-trained craftsmen, but at the same time provide new jobs never before imagined.

Development in technology have always changed the mix of labor and skills needed. Some areas will experience lower demand, and other areas will see impressive growth. Pay and benefits will vary widely depending on such demand and supply. Chinese optimists believe that even if singularity comes, there will be a solution and that the state has a particular responsibility to educate and provide for the people left outside. The Chinese pessimists echo the late Stephen Hawking and Elon Musk's warning of a possible quick demise of human kind. Wherever on the spectrum, you belong, most Beijing thinkers I speak to agree that China cannot afford to lose out to Washington or Tokyo in this race, and is hitting *"the pedal to the metal"* in the race fueling AI development with money and regulatory incentives.

Interestingly, US-China cross boarder AI investments is also heating up. From 2016 to 2017 China's investment to US AI start-ups increased from 19 to 31, while US-backed investment in Chinese AI startups increased from 5 to 20 in the same period. According to CB Insights, an international research consultancy, Chinese investments accounted for 48 percent of global AI startup funding and outstripped the USA in AI related patent publications. CB lists that China outdid the USA in intellectual property ("IP") filings for "deep learning" 652 compared with 101; for "artificial intelligence" 641 to 130 and for "machine learning" 882 to about 770. This is *not* conclusive evidence of a China lead but may help indicate the respective balance somewhat. It is my expectation nevertheless that Chinese AI businesses for reasons explained above may find it more easy to expand locally and to large emerging markets as compared to American firms.

Apart from capital, why will China succeed?
The key to AI is data. Lots of data. The more data you have, the smarter your AI technology can become. An analogy often used is that *"A good scientist with tons of data will beat a great scientist with only a small amount of data."* No one has "as much data," either on people or on "connected things" as China. So, if the analogy and thesis that data amount makes a difference in the development of AI, then China has an advantage. Data itself may determine which companies and countries will take the global lead in AI development.

So, how much data is China gathering, you may ask? I assume you, like us, have a gut feeling China has and generates more data than anyone. China has the most mobile phones and internet users in the world, nearly all using their mobile phones to pay for goods and services. The US and Europe do not come close. Chinese companies are in a position to develop smarter artificial intelligence faster than its international competitors merely on the back of monitoring and adjusting to these data sets on consumer behavior.

Most of China's technology companies share all or some data with Chinese government authorities to improve consumer trust online, while US tech giants Facebook and Google are blocked from the mainland. Such data sharing and government protection have provided a *"digital data lagoon"* that help local Chinese tech companies grow rapidly and experiment with AI. Since data is a *"scarce resource"* or a critical component for AI development, China has established near exclusive control over large data sets for its own private companies and government research institutes alike.

While China remains closed off, one could also argue that the Cambridge Analytica scandal in 2018 has caused general data backlash in the USA and Europe. The new General Data Protection Regulation (GDPR) standardizes data protection law across all 28 EU countries and imposes strict new rules on controlling and processing personally identifiable information ("PII"). There are many essential items in the regulation, including increased fines, breach notifications, opt-in consent and responsibility for data transfer outside the EU. As a result, the potential impact on western businesses may be huge and has permanently changed the way customer data is collected, stored and used.

Where GDRP policy is implemented to protect European internet users, China does not work in identical ways to Europe in protecting user privacy. Robin Li, the founder, and CEO of Baidu was quoted in Chinese media to have said that *"Chinese people are willing to use their privacy in exchange for convenience."* This is a common statement in China, yet caused dissatisfaction among some Chinese netizens at the time. Full disclosure of personal information is normal in China and is entirely unlikely to change. Li is correct in that most people in China, this author included, is more than willing to sacrifice personal data and usage patterns in exchange for security, safety, and convenience.

In China, the larger tech companies have volunteered to share all or most data usage with government authorities in exchange for licenses and government protection. In effect, bonds between Baidu, Alibaba, Tencent, and Sina ("BATS") and the Chinese government is closer than might be detected for the untrained eye. The BATS are way too powerful and important for the Beijing government not to indirectly or directly control the companies.

A market criticism is that the BATS are *too* powerful and *too* dominant, which they certainly are today. That said, they are successful because the Chinese government were helpful in developing a domestic tech sector, but also because they were innovative and came up with services that Chinese people want. To stay dominant, they will need to keep developing what Beijing and Chinese people want. There is little evidence in history that the big data and tech driven companies will remain dominant for that long. Nokia, Blackberry, Motorola, Kodak, Yahoo and Sony are all companies that were dominant in fields where today they are severely challenged or nearly forgotten. At the same time, the BATS are generous in feeding the tech ecosystem. Nearly half of all VC investments in China in 2017 originated from the BATS. This is a unique China aspect.

The Beijing State Council has singled out and listed a number of local companies to lead the AI development, including the BATS. Baidu is one of the leaders, trying to distance itself from a reputation as "the Chinese Google." Baidu's investor presentations label the company as an artificial intelligence company. I heard in Beijing that Baidu has about 2,700 engineers and PhDs working on AI from various locations. Meanwhile, at Alibaba, they AI focus seems to be centered on Alibaba Cloud and applying AI to various business scenarios, especially in smart retail and e-commerce.

Tencent is hosting about 55% of China's mobile internet usage on its platforms. Tencent's mission is to "become the most respected internet enterprise in the world." The company is China's biggest social network company with 1 billion users on its mobile app WeChat and with more than 650 million monthly user accounts. Tencent has publicly laid out its AI strategy based on three major scenarios: games, social interaction, and content. The game related AI applications circle around player experience and e-sports, where for example a character in a game world would start to "think for themselves" and be able to break away from a fixed character play. The idea is to have characters develop differently, into different scenarios and stories. Tencent is also active in several autonomous driving vehicle projects with partners like the Beijing Automotive Group (BAIC) and in healthcare/personalized medicine companies using AI. For example, thousands of hospitals and medical clinics allow their patients to book and pay through Tencent services, providing Tencent with primary data on users' health and preferences. Tencent has already launched virtual healthcare assistants that are able to communicate with their users on personalized medicine.

China's SenseTime became the most valuable AI startup in the world at US$ 4.5 billion when Alibaba led a US$600m fundraise in April 2018. SenseTime have solutions that identify your face, estimate your age and purchasing habits. A leader in facial recognition technologies, applying their AI to everything from traffic surveillance to employee authorization, SenseTime is one of 168 Chinese unicorns, collectively valued at over $628 billion.

In China one can now nearly on a daily basis read about criminals being arrested as face recognizing algorithms is matching faces entering buses, train stations, shopping malls or even concerts. Authorities are quickly dispatched to pick up suspects using technology that combine AI and facial-recognition capabilities. Facial recognition in China already goes far beyond opening your iPhone X or catching criminals. Many applications now are sensitive to your mood suggestion music to "pump you up," or demanding a smile to let you access your apps. Schools are using facial recognition to check and grade your attentiveness in class, arguably less arbitrary than any subjective teacher ever will.

Democratized large data sets, computing speed and volume, and a sense of urgency and hunger among government and entrepreneurs are separating factors in China's favor. It is time to kick out the thought of China as a copycat of the west. China is now the place to be to copy local Chinese companies or to develop your own tech with available local talent.

It is a brave new world indeed.

CHAPTER 2 – CHINESE BLOCKCHAIN

The cryptocurrency Bitcoin came to life on November 1, 2008. A computer programmer working under the pseudonym "Satoshi Nakamoto" that Saturday sent an email to a cryptography mailing list that he had created a "new peer to peer electronic cash system." A new asset class and a new technology was born.

Few paid initial attention, but in 2009 the first transactions were completed on what Nakamoto called a "block chain system" (Nakamoto wrote "block chain," but this has later become "blockchain"). The following grew "slowly, but surely" as the blockchain system seemed to work. Today it is a currency, and you ignore it at your own peril. This author has gone from a non-believer to a careful convert of the currency, while China has taken an opposite stance. While the Chinese government seems to have fully embraced the blockchain technology, it is doing all it can to block cryptocurrencies ("crypto"). China now bans so-called "mining," most cryptocurrencies itself and also the exchanges trading them. Most recent updates from Beijing is that now also events, news sites and foreign trading of cryptocurrencies for Chinese nationals is banned. _The reasons are obvious:_ the crypto market is full of fraud, Ponzi schemes and favored tools for illegal transfers.

Initially, so many Chinese got on the "bitcoin" train that in 2017 near 90% of trading in the cryptocurrency Bitcoin originated from China. So popular indeed that in September 2017, the People's Bank of China banned both Chinese exchanges and so-called "initial coin offerings" ("ICO") in China. China deems ICOs to be an "illegal public finance" mechanism suited to money laundering and the illegal issuance of securities. Chinese investors had since tried to move to offshore exchanges until February 2018, when the Chinese government also banned any activity related to foreign trade and exchange of cryptocurrencies.

China has historically been the dominant bitcoin miner, but early 2018 China's government released plans to shut down Bitcoin miners. Beijing has asked local governments to cause an "orderly exit" of Chinese miners from the industry. "Mining" which we will talk more about under, involves an energy-intensive process of solving math problems to complete transactions. Another official concern includes energy usage related to mining, with total annual electricity usage estimated at about 4 gigawatts of electricity (about 3 nuclear reactors). In April 2018, Chinese police stormed a large-scale Bitcoin mining operation in Tianjin city. Over 600 computers were confiscated in the raid where the government claimed that the operation was one of the largest power theft cases in China. This is only one of many, many such interventions.

Beijing's concern related to cryptocurrencies is related to the Ponzi schemes, fraud, money laundering and illegal transfer of assets that so many cryptocurrencies and ICO's represent. However, China seems convinced that the underlying technology called blockchain has value, especially beyond the use of blockchain related to currencies. As for currency, it would not surprise this author if at some point Beijing allows for some form of homemade, domestically regulated crypto market and currency. At this point, no one knows.

In order to bring all readers up to a level playing field, I wanted to sketch some of the main differences between bitcoins and blockchain. This way you and I can discuss if it has value or not. Ok? Kaiche!

What is difference between bitcoin and blockchain?

The simplest way I know to describe the difference between bitcoin and blockchain is that blockchain is the operating system and bitcoins is an application running on that operating system.

Bitcoin is one of many cryptocurrencies, but arguably the most successful one (but banned in China). There are many other cryptocurrencies, some of them also successful, including "Ethereum" and "Litecoins." However, in this author's personal opinion, the vast majority of cryptocurrencies are scams, Ponzi schemes and have no or little value. I will here focus on Bitcoins, but please be reminded that Bitcoin is not representative for most current cryptos. Most of them are awful.

A bitcoin is an attempt at creating digital money. It has worked since 2008 with relatively few problems. "Money" has come in many forms over millenniums: from shells, salt, tulips, goats, gold, silver and most recently various government *paper*. They have all had their distinct problems. Owning a goat or a Venezuelan bolivar may not be the best storage of value, will you not agree? At least the goat may be difficult to use if you trade in e-commerce with another continent, and the Bolivar has been in free fall for years. Let's at least agree they are a challenging and high maintenance place to store value, typically requiring face to face delivery or a trusted intermediary.

Bitcoin is enabled by computing technology. It does *not* require "face to face" delivery and is owned by the people, *not* requiring a trusted intermediary. Digital payments have until now needed an intermediary, or one would be subject to open-ended double spending (the digital units being copied uncontrollably). A trusted intermediary has been needed to verify that one unit previously owned by you is now owned by another. Bitcoin eliminates this risk and necessity through a distributed ledger system.

A distributed ledger is a database held by different computing devices or nodes. Each node holds an identical copy of the ledger. The participating nodes in the network updates itself independently and keeps track of "which addresses own what." The nodes "vote" on updates to the ledger, without the participation of a central authority.

With Bitcoin, you do not need to carry paper in your wallet to hand over physically to anyone. To further understand this, let us look at the mining process and the blockchain concept.

What is mining?
Crypto "mining" is a just a borrowed term from digging for precious metals, but there is no dirt and digging involved here. Nakamoto created a distributed peer to peer ledger where every transaction has to be recorded by every member of the network. Whenever there is a transfer, all the members have to verify that there is sufficient balance for the transfer and the members *compete* to be the first to update the ledger with a new block of transactions every ten minutes. To confirm the transaction, the member has to solve a difficult, but easily verifiable mathematical problem, for which the member will need computing power and electricity.

Once a member/node has solved the so-called "proof of work" correctly, and a majority of the other nodes in the network votes for its validity, then that node is awarded a "block" of bitcoins added to the supply of bitcoins. This is what mining is, and the "block" is the "gold."

The block is the reward for spending time to build computer centers with processing power and paying salaries and the electricity bills for computing. In a traditional paper money system, the government print money to pay for pensions or bridges. We can say "money is printed or dug out" by those who spend resources verifying the transactions. This system is key to the applications running on the ledger, and the ledger or blockchain itself.

As opposed to Bolivars or dollars, there is a limit to the supply of Bitcoins. Nakamoto not only set a limit to the upper supply at 21 million coins, but the mining blocks came down from 50 every 10 minutes, first to 25 and then halved every four years. This should, *in theory,* increase the value of both holding and mining bitcoins. Mining bitcoins will become more and more costly: remember the reward is halved every four years, as the miners have to spend more resources on solving the problems. There also is a *difficulty adjustment* in the code, accounting for improved processing power.

The above is possibly the most beautiful aspect of this new asset class. Think about it: in any other asset class, as the value increases, the efforts to find and produce it will even be higher. The higher the value of oil or gold, the more we will mine, and the less profitable reserves will now be exploited. If the value of oil falls, difficult to access reserves will be left unexplored. The more valuable gold or oil is, the more incentivized we are to mine and the more we will exploit the earth, for example by exploring in the Arctic oceans.

The supply curve for Bitcoins grew sharply from about zero in 2009 to about 6 million in 2011 to about 18 million now, and will stay flat forever at 21 million from about 2024. For Bitcoins, a higher value of the asset does not lead to more supply. Supply is fixed. Meanwhile, the processing power needed to commit to valid transactions will increase, and the network becomes more secure. The growth in value cannot increase growth in supply. No one can decide to start to mine and find more Bitcoins. The safety increases because to solve the "mathematical problem" require a lot of resources, while it costs nearly nothing to verify. Hence, a lot of work can be rejected by little effort from the group. The verification is near effortless and not dependent on a third party.

Dishonesty in the process would cost a lot, and be rejected at near zero cost. The majority is not rewarded to be dishonest, as *if* they were dishonest then the entire value proposition would collapse to nothing. Cheating to get a block would render the block and any balance held worthless. Fraud is costly, and no member can alter the ledger alone, especially not a central bank. Bitcoins, through the underlying blockchain technology, is not only scarce, but supply is *absolutely* fixed.

From 2009 it was enough to let a laptop process the computations for mining, but as time progressed more powerful hardware was required. Application specific integrated circuits (ASIC) computer chip cards were developed from 2015, specifically for mining bitcoin, changing the industry. The mining servers are usually put into mining "farms" which is just large datacenters constructed to mine cryptocurrencies. In the centers, there are various solutions, as the miners can choose to pool their interest or go solo. A mining pool puts together all the resources in the given pool and distributes the mined bitcoins, a solo miner performs the operations alone and therefore slightly reduces the chances of mining a block, but also increases the payout if a block should be mined. Upon receiving bitcoins, the miners can send them to a bitcoin exchange and sell them. Truly amazing "Klondike" like stories have come out of these farms and still do.

China status

China has and in many ways still is at the epicenter of the Bitcoin both in terms of mining, trading, and storage. One of the biggest miners in the world is Beijing-based company Bitmain with an estimated private market capitalization of US$12 billion and a reported revenue of US$2.5 billion in 2017. The revenue mainly came from selling ASIC semiconductors and revenue share mining pools. Bitmain owns two large mining pools called BTC.com and AntPool, together accounting for an estimated 35% all the bitcoin mined in the world. Many critics are concerned about Bitmain's ownership of these large mining pools and their ability to manipulate outcomes. In total, it is estimated that China performed about 60% of the total mining in 2016, mainly from Inner Mongolia, Xinjiang, Sichuan, and Yunnan where electricity and land were cheap. The miners are now on the way from China to other locations, including Hong Kong, Singapore, and Taiwan, but also Iceland, Norway or other locations with low electricity costs.

The People's Bank of China is entirely unlikely to ever allow private parties to issue their own currency, as it undermines any government's ability to fund itself. Governments have always been tempted to issue more paper, especially when their paper money is worth a lot. When the Chinese government banned Chinese exchanges and domestic trading of bitcoins, it was a shock to the system. Bitcoins dropped nearly 40% in September 2017, before quickly recovering. By the end of the year, Bitcoins had doubled from where it was before the Chinese ban. As trading in China of Bitcoins came down, it is likely that most Chinese have shifted strategy to hold Bitcoins *for the longer term*. This should be beneficial to the long-term value of bitcoins.

Bitcoins is unlikely to become a mass distributed solution for micro-payments, like WeChat wallets or even debit/credit cards.

The need for the entire ledger to be updated with each transaction prevents Bitcoin to become a permanent payment solution. Quite simply, the processing cost and time to update the ledger is prohibitive. For example, it can take up to 10-15 minutes for a transaction to be confirmed, which is far too long if you are buying a coffee at Starbucks with bitcoins. For micro payments, centralized solutions like Visa or MasterCard are better. Hence, Bitcoins are more suited for long-term storage of value.

Distributed ledger and blockchain
No, they are *not* the same. Distributed ledgers are not all blockchain, but all blockchains are distributed ledgers. Blockchain technology is a form of distributed ledger technology, but not exactly the same as some distributed ledgers do not employ a chain of blocks to provide a secure and valid distributed consensus.

As described above, Bitcoin uses a distributed ledger technology, also referred to as "DLT." All data on a *blockchain* is grouped together and organized in blocks that are linked to one another and secured using cryptography. A blockchain, therefore, is a growing list of records where data is continuously added to a database and verified. Altering or deleting previously entered data on earlier blocks is impossible. Blockchain technology is custom made for recording events, managing records, processing transactions, and tracing assets.

Remember that the ledger is controlled by the majority of its users, giving those bodies control together. Put like that, it does not sound so "decentralized" anymore, does it? Ledger updates require the majority of nodes to agree. Such "consensus" cause the distributed ledger to update itself and the latest, version of the ledger is then saved on each node separately. I earlier mentioned that there is an economic incentive for the majority not to compromise Bitcoins distributed ledger system as it could cause the entire value to evaporate. The risk of 51% of the nodes to cooperate *against* the minority, does seem to be a weakness of the distributed ledger technology. It opens up for attacks at the currency from participants that may have ulterior motives, like a nation state looking to bring down the ledger or currency permanently.

Blockchain is in China deployed in multiple sectors, other than currencies, for example, to reduce the number of counterfeit invoices. Counterfeit invoices can be filed as business expenses, reducing tax liabilities. In a ground breaking project, the Chinese Tax Bureau in Shenzhen and Tencent has collaborated to create a blockchain invoice system that protects the authenticity of the invoices. To ensure the authenticity, the system will keep a comprehensive log of data on the issuers and recipients. This allows the tax authorities to inspect, verify and track invoices.

As of June 2018, the system has commenced operation in parts of Guangzhou. In 2017, data from the World Intellectual Property Organization shows that 406 blockchain patents were filed, with over 225 of these patents belonged to China. The second biggest filer of blockchain patents was the US at 95. China's president Xi refers to blockchain a breakthrough technology with vast implementation of blockchain projects now executed on a provincial level all over China. Several Chinese smart city projects have procured the Ethereum blockchain technology, which is underlying and running the Ethereum cryptocurrency. It seems like many Chinese cities are looking to be the first adopters of blockchain in the world, not copying anyone, rather setting a new standard.

Keeping it in perspective

While grabbing global market attention, cryptocurrencies ("crypto") represent only a minuscule portion of global assets. Putting cryptos in perspective, as of mid-year 2018, the five largest cryptocurrencies merely accounted for US$200 billion in total market capitalization or merely half the Norwegian "Gross Domestic Product" (GDP). As a yard stick, Norway's GPD was 398.83 billion US dollars in 2017 or 0.64 percent of the world GDP. The total global crypto currency market was estimated by experts to be about US$ 250 billion dollars mid-2018. That is nothing. Bitcoin accounted for nearly 50% of that market capitalization, falling sharply since peak prices in December 2017. The second largest currency was Ethereum with about US$ 41 billion dollars in market cap or about 80% of the value of Tesla.

Compared to other major global assets, cryptocurrencies are insignificant: The global stock market mid-2018 was valued around US$ 100 trillion and the global real estate market is valued at nearly 250 trillion dollars. Another favored storage of value, gold is globally valued at above 10 trillion dollars.

Bitcoin is truly insignificant as compared to other means of storing value. Before the January 2018 collapse, the total crypto market cap was around US$800 billion. But again, by comparison, Apple Incs market cap soared above US$1 trillion this year; the Shanghai Stock Exchange reached a market cap of US$4.5 trillion, and the Shenzhen Stock Exchange's market cap was US$3.1 trillion around the same time. Cryptos are not a major global "currency" as compared to stocks, real estate, cash, derivatives or even gold. Still, cryptos have something that other assets do not have: intangibility and possible anonymity. Market hype caused cryptocurrency to soar, until the Chinese government intervention in 2017 and 2018, which we have seen caused a rapid fall.

A rare phenomenon for Bitcoin is that while they all have unique, distributed digital address, it is entirely possible to lose a Bitcoin and no one will ever be able to access it, and you will never get it back. If you send it to the wrong address, there is no way of retrieving it. If you store your bitcoins on a hard drive and lose that hard drive, then the bitcoins are gone. Forever. Not only do you lose them, but now they are also out of circulation, increasing the intrinsic value of the outstanding volumes.

There are numerous stories of individuals that have mined or acquired Bitcoins for later to lose them all. Since there is no central authority controlling Bitcoin, there is no one who can help you retrieve them if you lose them. So, if you lose your private address key, you effectively reduce the total supply of bitcoins in the world. It is estimated that between 2.78 million and 3.79 million bitcoins are completely lost and out of circulation permanently. That means that between 17 percent and 23 percent of the total Bitcoin supply is lost. With a maximum total supply of 21 million bitcoins, lost bitcoins will always be a significant variable of the total pool. The more is lost, the higher the value of each single bitcoin will be. It is possible but unlikely that the current reduced total supply is fully factored into the Bitcoin price. No one knows, and this is not one of the most attractive aspects of cryptos.

No one also knows exactly how much Bitcoins is held by Chinese households or institutions, but as mentioned above, Chinese renminbi trading has historically been between 50% and 90% of the bitcoin trading volume in the world. Trading does not reflect *holding* of course, as there may be a major dislocation between traders and holders, also through the so-called "bitcoin whales." Bitcoin whales are thought to be about 1,000 investors that hold more than 40% of the total volume outstanding of bitcoins. However, many of the whales trading can be traced back to the

Chinese crypto exchanges pointing to that many of the whales could indeed be Chinese. The whales are feared, as if they were to conduct a sell off then the market would plummet uncontrollably. This concentration of ownership itself is making governments and investors wary of the asset. A complicating factor is that some institutions or individuals may also control different ledger addresses and as such have even larger positions than what we are assuming today. All of this speculation is unhelpful and contributes to an asset that is not seen as stable or as too volatile.

Who regulates this market and blockchain in China?

If you ask this question in China, you will get many different answers. Most agree that the People's Bank of China ("PBOC") is the largest influencer and initiates regulations. Cryptocurrencies started out unregulated in China and were tradable for the public up to September 2017 when so-called initial coin offerings ("ICOs") were deemed illegal, and mainland cryptocurrency exchanges were ordered to shut down.

In January 2018, further measurements were taken, and local governments started to take action towards cryptocurrency-mining operations in their jurisdiction. In February 2018, the PBOC announced that overseas cryptocurrency exchanges would also be banned. The PBOC, however, have historically been quite bullish on digital currencies and has stated that they are working on a state regulated Chinese digital currency. The PBOC has an own cryptocurrency research department called the "Digital Currency Research Lab." The PBOC lab is busy submitting cryptocurrency patents, having submitted more than 40 patents half way into 2018 alone.

The Chinese State Council has supported setting up a variety of expert panels and committees on digital currencies, including the

National Committee of Experts on the Internet Financial Security Technology, or IFCERT. IFCERT is an industry organization backed by the Chinese government. IFCERT consists of internet financial security experts that also was involved in the 2018 crackdown on mining. The shutdown of both the mining process and the many exchanges was initiated by the PBOC, yet executed by local governments.

Chinese speculation
China, like many if not most countries has an uneven distribution of wealth. The poorest 25% of the Chinese population own only 1% of the aggregate wealth in China. Income varies hugely between the provinces, resulting in uneven development and traders looking for fast returns. Cryptocurrencies have since conception been associated with illegalities and *"getting rich quick"* schemes.

This is a global phenomenon, not only Chinese. That said, China may have been disproportionately over represented with IFCERT itself reporting over 500 fake cryptocurrencies to date, many running from Europe and the USA, but aggressively marketed in China. One such infamous crypto was "OneCoin," a crypto run from Bulgaria that was later cracked down upon from Beijing with more than 100 people now being prosecuted in Beijing alone. There is no telling what is a scam and what may be legit, with many investors choosing either to stay completely out or hedging bets by going as *"wide as possible"* in their holdings. Most value-driven investors are keeping out altogether.

Robbery and hacking
A well-known cryptocurrency exchange collapse was Japan's Mt. Gox, which from 2013 to the beginning of 2014 it was the largest Bitcoin exchange in the world. Mt. Gox then reportedly handled nearly 70% of all the transactions worldwide. Mt. Gox had seen a

large number of bitcoins stolen by cyber thieves, and this raised rightfully many critical questions from regulators. Mt. Gox went under with all bitcoins disappearing and no holder having received any form of reimbursement. If the exchange holding your coins goes bankrupt, alas, so goes your coins. Today, a prominent exchange is San Francisco based Coinbase, and should this exchange disappear, so may the coins of Coinbase clients. Obviously, this is a major risk for holders. There is no uniform international regulation in place for cryptos, and it is up to the country where the cryptocurrency exchange is situated to decide what happens in the case of bankruptcy. So far, it is muddy waters.

Final thoughts
When arrived to Beijing in the 1990's, China was in the past, labeled as a "copycat." China was looking outward for inspiration and know-how. It did so very successfully.

Now, China is already in the future. Pushed forward by funding and research from the central government, China AI seems unbeatable. My recommendation is that you and your company have to be here to take part or expose yourselves to this development. Ignoring China AI development could be a serious board room or parliamentary mistake. Investors, consumers, companies and governments all over the world must stop to think of China as a copycat nation, come here and take part in the innovative, rapid and continuous transformation.

I finish on the words of comedian Conan O'Brien: *"A new survey shows that 1 in 5 Americans believe that God steers the global economy. Mystery solved: God is Chinese."*

ACKNOWLEDGEMENTS

First and foremost, I want to thank my interns Sindre Laksemo and Monica Liu. They spent the better part of summer 2018 reading and looking into this topic with me. I only regret not spending more time with them, but their work has been essential for this work. Both of you will go far in China, I am sure. Good luck.

Second, I want to thank the amazing individuals, teams and positive *"can do attitudes"* at nHack Ventures, especially Jon Eivind Stø and Li Peng.

Also a huge thank you the amazing people at Danske Bank, WeWork, Antler, the Norwegian Embassy and Consulates in China, Business Sweden, Innovation Norway, Innovation Centre Denmark, Business Finland, Nordic Innovation House, Wikborg Rein, Investinor, Lingang and not least NTNU TTO.

Finally, also want to thank my friends around House of Tech, Techbuddy and Reachtail in Stockholm. You are all amazing and it has been unforgettable to work with you during 2018. Keep on being the greatest.

Chris Rynning

REFERENCES

12th Five-Year Plan (2011-2015) for National Economic and Social Development | ESCAP Policy Documents Management. Xinhua News Agency, China's National People's Congress, 2011, www.gov.cn

Clover, Charles and Ju, Sherry. "China tech groups to share data with state in online fraud battle." October 26, 2016. Accessed December 7, 2017.

He, Yujia. "How China Is Preparing for an AI-Powered Future." Wilson Center, 26 July. 2017.

Ji, Zhenyu. "FB stock price plummeted triggered technology stock panic", Tencent Shenwang, August. 2018,

Lee, Kai-fu, and Paul Triolo. "China Embraces AI: A Close Look and A Long View." Eurasia Group, Dec. 2017

Lee, Kaifu. "A blueprint for the coexistence of human and artificial intelligence." Zhigu news, July. 2017, http://zhigu.news.cn/2017-07/12/c_129654643.htm

Mozur, Paul. "Beijing Wants A.I. to Be Made in China by 2030." The New York Times, 20th July. 2017

Moore, Mike. "What is AI? Everything you need to know." Techradar. pro, 1st August 2018

Natural Sciences Sector. "China: Taking Stock of Progress towards Becoming an Innovation-Driven Nation | United Nations Educational, Scientific and Cultural Organization." UNESCO, Discovery Channel, Producer., Feb. 2016

"Rise of China's Big Tech In AI: What Baidu, Alibaba, And Tencent Are Working On", CBsights, April. 2018

Wang, Jinxu, "Tencent releases AI strategy: Make AI everywhere", Leiphone net, November. 2017

What Is General Data Protection Regulation? Forbes, Feb. 2018

Zhang Yi, "What is the difference between BAT companies." 36kr.com, July. 2017.

https://qz.com/1313477/top-500-supercomputers-china-is-far-ahead-of-the-us-in-its-share-of-the-top-machines/

https://www.investopedia.com/news/bitcoin-banned-china/

https://www.investopedia.com/news/china-plans-crack-down-international-cryptocurrency-trading-its-citizens/

https://www.forbes.com/sites/pamelaambler/2018/02/07/changpeng-zhao-binance-exchange-crypto-cryptocurrency/#5cac808d1eee

www.ingramcontent.com/pod-product-compliance
Lightning Source LLC
Chambersburg PA
CBHW031249050326
40690CB00007B/1019